Biggest UPSETS in Sports

by
Ken Rappoport

Published by ABDO Publishing Company, PO Box 398166, Minneapolis, MN 55439. Copyright © 2014 by Abdo Consulting Group, Inc. International copyrights reserved in all countries. No part of this book may be reproduced in any form without written permission from the publisher. SportsZone™ is a trademark and logo of ABDO Publishing Company.

Printed in the United States of America,
North Mankato, Minnesota
052013
092013

Editor: Chrös McDougall
Series Designer: Craig Hinton

Photo Credits: AP Images, cover, 1, 12, 17, 19, 41, 42, 49, 54; John Kelly/Getty Images, 5; Steve Powell/Getty Images, 9; Lois Bernstein/AP Images, 11; Kevin Reece/AP Images, 14; NFL Photos/AP Images, 20; Tom DiPace/AP Images, 23; Ross D. Franklin/AP Images, 25; Ted S. Warren/AP Images, 27; Katsumi Kasahara/AP Images, 29; J. Pat Carter/AP Images, 31; Lionel Cironneau/AP Images, 32; Tsugufumi Matsumoto/AP Images, 37; Ronald C. Modra/Sports Imagery/Getty Images, 39; Gary Landers/AP Images, 45; Steve Moore Archives/AP Images, 51; J. Walter Green/AP Images, 56; Elise Amendola/AP Images, 59

Library of Congress Control Number: 2013932583

Cataloging-in-Publication Data
Rappoport, Ken.
 Biggest upsets in sports / Ken Rappoport.
  p. cm. -- (Sports' biggest moments)
ISBN 978-1-61783-923-8
Includes bibliographical references and index.
1. Sports upsets--Juvenile literature. 2. Sports--Miscellanea--Juvenile literature. I. Title.
796--dc23
                                                                    2013932583

TABLE OF CONTENTS

Chapter 1   Great Team Upsets 4

Chapter 2   Great Football Upsets 16

Chapter 3   Great Individual Upsets 28

Chapter 4   Great Basketball Upsets 38

Chapter 5   Great Baseball Upsets 50

Fun Facts 60
Glossary 61
For More Information 62
Index 64
About the Author 64

GREAT TEAM UPSETS

The winter of 1980 was a time of despair and hardship in the United States. Jobs were hard to find. Iran held 52 US citizens hostage. Their tired faces were on television every night. Soviet troops invaded Afghanistan. It threatened world peace. The powerful United States suddenly seemed weak.

Along came a group made up mostly of college kids. It was the US Olympic hockey team. National Hockey League (NHL) players were not allowed to play in the Olympic Winter Games until 1998. So these amateurs from around the country would have to do. Meanwhile, the Soviet Union had the most dominant team in the world. Just the year before the Soviets had beaten an NHL All-Star team.

Team USA coach Herb Brooks worked his players hard. In fact, he worked them so hard and so long that the players hated him. But that

Team USA goalie Jim Craig blocks a shot against the Soviet Union during their game at the 1980 Olympic Winter Games.

was all part of the plan. This group of amateurs was being prepared to face the best hockey team in the world. Brooks hoped the brutally hard work would unite the team before the 1980 Winter Games in Lake Placid, New York.

The Americans went on a grueling 61-game pre-Olympic tour, playing night after night. They developed confidence. Then, a few weeks before the Winter Games, Brooks scheduled his team to play the Soviets in a practice game in New York. The result was unsurprising. The Soviets crushed the Americans 10–3. When the Olympics finally began, expectations were low for Team USA.

"We realized we were immense underdogs," Brooks said, "but that reality sort of lit the competitive fires."

That showed when Team USA arrived in Lake Placid. Night after night, the team would rally to win or tie. The opening game was against a powerful Sweden team. The Americans were losing 2–1 with only 27 seconds left. Then a 55-foot shot by Bill Baker tied the game at 2–2. Team USA was tied 2–2 with Czechoslovakia after one period in the second game. Then the Americans pulled away to win 7–3. Team USA trailed in two of its next three games as well. But the Americans rallied to win each one. Suddenly the United States found itself in the medal round.

The 1980 Olympics had a unique medal round. There was no single-elimination bracket. Instead the top two teams from both preliminary groups were put in a final group. Then each team would play the two teams from the other preliminary group. For the United States, that meant games against the Soviet Union and Finland.

"The locker room was somber, quiet, no panic," Brooks said of the game against the Soviets.

Once again, however, the Americans were trailing their opponents early. They were having a difficult time holding off the Soviets. It appeared that the first period would end with the Soviets leading 2–1. Suddenly, American Mark Johnson came out of the blue. With one second left on the clock, he scored a goal off a rebound. The Soviet coach was so mad he pulled legendary goalie Vladislav Tretiak.

The momentum quickly changed to the Americans' side. "It was unbelievable," US defenseman Jack O'Callahan said.

Their confidence did not fade when the Soviets went ahead 3–2 in the second period. After all, the Americans were known as the "Comeback Kids." In the third period, Johnson tied the game with another close-range shot. Then less than two minutes later Mike Eruzione put Team USA ahead with a long wrist shot. Meanwhile, US goalie Jim Craig played the game of his life, making 36 often-spectacular saves throughout the game.

In the closing minutes, with the United States up 4–3, the crowd was chanting, "U-S-A! U-S-A!" As the clock wound down, fans started to count, "Ten, nine, eight . . . " Almost hysterical, broadcaster Al Michaels raised his voice to a much higher pitch.

"Do you believe in miracles?" he shouted over the stadium's rising noise. Then he answered himself. "Yes!"

The buzzer went off. The Americans had a 4–3 win. Many consider "The Miracle on Ice" to be the greatest upset of all time. The victory did not secure the gold medal, though. The United States did not claim that until two days later. Once again the Americans went down against Finland. And once again they came back to win.

Suddenly, Americans were feeling better about themselves and the future of their country.

Miracle on Grass

Uruguay won the 1950 World Cup, but arguably the most famous game in the tournament came two weeks earlier in the preliminary round.

The United States was playing England. The two teams could not have been further apart. Soccer in its modern form was invented in England. The English undoubtedly had some of the best soccer players, too.

The US players celebrate after beating the Soviet Union in what became known as "The Miracle on Ice."

And although England was playing in its first World Cup in 1950, most people considered England to be among the favorites to win it all.

The Americans were hardly soccer powers. In fact they were hardly on the soccer radar. Although soccer had once thrived in parts of the United States, it was very much in the sporting background by 1950. Nonetheless, the Americans put together a team. Not one of the players was famous. They were a working-class group of World War II veterans. The players had grown up playing soccer, but none had played at the top professional level of the English players. In fact, few people in the United States even knew that a US team was in Brazil for the World Cup.

Not much was expected from Team USA at the 1994 World Cup. The host team didn't have the talent or experience to be a contender. Instead, organizers hoped the tournament could boost soccer's popularity in the United States by bringing in the world's best teams and players. One of those teams was Colombia. Team USA and Colombia met in their second game at the Rose Bowl in Pasadena, California. Afterward, the US players refused to leave the field. They had wrapped themselves in American flags as the crowd roared "U-S-A." The Americans had won 2–1. "We shocked the world, we shocked the world!" shouted US striker Earnie Stewart. He scored the winning goal. The win helped the United States advance to the second round of the tournament.

The United States was 500-to-1 underdogs. The English were looking ahead to an easy time against the Americans in the group-stage match. The Americans? They just wanted to put in a good performance. They didn't think they had a chance.

When the game began, the Americans found unlikely support from the home crowd. Brazil was also a favorite to win the World Cup. So the local fans cheered for the Americans to beat England.

What happened next was entirely expected. For the first 30 minutes, "[The English] were all over us," said Harry Keough, who had worked as a mailman. "They had complete dominance, almost as if we were just watching them play."

Despite their dominance, the English couldn't score a goal. Suddenly the unexpected happened. Walter Bahr, a high school teacher, struck a shot from out on the right. The English goalkeeper had it covered. Not so fast.

Enter Joe Gaetjens, a 26-year-old dishwasher whom the coach didn't want on the team. He deflected the shot from Bahr into the net. The goal put the United States up 1–0. The 10,151 Brazilians in the stadium cheered wildly.

The English seemed shocked. They put the pressure on even more, hoping to find the back of the net. With eight minutes left, England's Stan Mortensen was about to score a goal. At least it looked that way. Instead, Charlie Colombo tackled the English player. England had a free kick.

Brazilian fans carry US forward Joe Gaetjens off the field after the United States beat England in the 1950 World Cup.

Frank Borghi was the US goalkeeper. As the ball went by his hand, he stretched, reached behind and flipped the ball out. The English were upset and protested that the ball was over the goal line. It wasn't.

The Americans held on to win. The 1–0 score was so unbelievable that the *New York Times* held off printing. Editors at the *Times* thought the score must have been 10–1 in England's favor. The game was not on TV so they had no way to verify, so the editors figured it had been recorded wrong.

The United States lost its remaining group-stage game to Chile and was eliminated. But the team had already pulled off the greatest upset in World Cup history.

The Miracle on Manchester

The Los Angeles Kings were happy just to make the NHL playoffs. It was 1982, and their first opponent just happened to be the most powerful offensive team in hockey history: the Edmonton Oilers.

With Wayne Gretzky leading the way, the Oilers seemed unbeatable. In the 1981–82 season they led the league with 417 goals. Said Kings forward Charlie Simmer, "We were outclassed, out-talented, out-everythinged."

No one could imagine the Oilers losing to the Kings. What a surprise when the Kings won the opening game 10–8. It was the most goals ever scored in a Stanley Cup playoff game.

No problem. The Oilers would get back on track in Game 2. And they did, with a 3–2 overtime win on a goal by Gretzky.

Game 3 started badly for the Kings. It was 5–0 after two periods. "Boo" shouted their fans as the Kings left the ice. On their return, "Boo" shouted the Oilers, laughing and jeering. Kings owner Jerry Buss gave up on his team. He left during the third period.

"The feeling was, 'Let's not make it 10–0,'" said Kings forward Jim Fox.

The younger players were not ready to give in.

"We were willing to go in and give it our best shot," said Daryl Evans, a rookie forward that season for the Kings.

GLORY FOR GRANATO

Growing up in Chicago, Cammi Granato wanted to play for the NHL's Chicago Blackhawks. There was one problem: she was a girl. That didn't stop Granato from playing hockey, though. She became a pioneer for women's hockey. And when women's hockey was added to the Olympic Winter Games in 1998, Granato was Team USA's captain and star. Canada was the heavy favorite to win the first gold medal. After all, the Canadians had beaten the Americans at four straight world championships. But in a shocker, Granato and Team USA beat Canada 3–1 in the gold-medal game.

It was the third period when Jay Wells scored a Kings goal. It was only the second time he scored all season. The TV camera panned to the Oilers bench. Their players were still smiling. After all, it was still 5–1. Then a power play goal made it 5–2. The Oilers bench was no longer laughing. Owner Buss was on his way home listening to the car radio when the Kings made it 5–3. The Kings scored two more goals to tie the game at 5–5. The game would be decided in overtime.

With a couple of minutes gone, the teams lined up for a faceoff. The Kings won the draw. The puck slid between the legs of Doug Smith to Evans in the right circle. The rookie cocked his left arm and fired a shot that sailed over goaltender Grant Fuhr's shoulder. The Kings won!

The 6–5 victory capped one of the greatest comebacks in Stanley Cup playoff history. Some called it a "miracle." Or precisely, they called it "The Miracle on Manchester," where the Kings' arena was located. The Kings won the series.

Chapter 2

GREAT FOOTBALL UPSETS

Joe Namath was a brash quarterback from Pennsylvania who found himself in the middle of a revolution. It was the 1960s. The upstart American Football League (AFL) was challenging the National Football League (NFL) for supremacy. The long-established NFL had always had the best teams. But now there was a bidding war for the top college talent in the United States.

Namath had led the University of Alabama to the 1964 national title. Naturally the NFL wanted to have him in the league. But in an astonishing deal, the AFL offered Namath his first football contract. News raced across the country: the New York Jets had signed Namath to a $427,000 deal. It was the largest in pro football history. That got the NFL's attention.

The AFL was known as a quarterbacks' league. It featured wide-open offenses with plenty of passing. The NFL was more conservative.

New York Jets quarterback Joe Namath gets a pass off under pressure during Super Bowl III.

UPSET IN THE BIG HOUSE

It was the opener of the 2007 football season. University of Michigan coach Lloyd Carr couldn't believe his eyes. Nor could the 110,000 fans at the stadium called "The Big House." Michigan was actually losing to Appalachian State University. The Wolverines were college football's all-time winningest team with a well-known history. Appalachian State? It was a small school, ignored by the major programs. Now it was being noticed. With six seconds left, the Mountaineers led by two points. Michigan quarterback Chad Henne had completed a 46-yard pass to Appalachian's 20-yard line. All the fifth-ranked Wolverines needed was a field goal to win it. The kick was blocked and returned to the 18. Game over. "We're still sort of shocked," Appalachian State coach Jerry Moore said after the 34–32 victory.

Namath, like the AFL, opted to do his own thing. He expressed his individuality. He was brash and colorful. He liked to wear fancy clothes, especially fur coats. He dated movie stars. He starred in a panty hose commercial. On the field, he was well-known for his trademark white shoes.

"Broadway Joe" was just the kind of quarterback the AFL needed to challenge the NFL.

By 1966, it was clear to both the AFL and the NFL that they would work better together. So the leagues merged into one. The merger would not be complete until 1970. But starting with the 1966 season, the AFL and NFL champions would play each other in a season-ending championship game. It would become known as the Super Bowl.

The Super Bowl technically put the AFL and NFL on equal footing. But few considered the two leagues equal. The long-established NFL

New York Jets quarterback Joe Namath hands the ball off to Matt Snell during Super Bowl III.

appeared to be the superior league. And indeed the NFL champion Green Bay Packers had beaten the AFL champions in the first two Super Bowls.

After the 1968 season, Namath led his Jets to Super Bowl III. But once again, the AFL champion was considered a huge underdog. The NFL champion Baltimore Colts were unbeaten in their last 10 games. Going into the Super Bowl, the Colts were favored to win by 18 points. As long as the Colts showed up, most people believed, they would win.

This frustrated Namath. So in a spur-of-the-moment remark before the Super Bowl, he "guaranteed" the Jets would win. Namath didn't know his guarantee would become a big deal. But that outrageous statement was the big story as the game kicked off.

The thought going into the game was that the Colts' strong defense would overwhelm the Jets. But Namath led a balanced attack of passing and running. And it was the Jets' defense that proved to be dominant. In the third quarter the AFL champions held a 13–0 lead.

The Colts were getting desperate. Late in the third quarter they pulled quarterback Earl Morrall in favor of sore-armed Johnny Unitas. It proved to be too little, too late. The Jets held on to win 16–7. A crowd of 75,377 at the Orange Bowl stadium in South Florida and 60 million more watching on TV were stunned.

Namath had fulfilled his guarantee. The Jets had proved that they could play with anyone in the NFL. When the AFL champion Kansas City Chiefs won Super Bowl IV the next year, it was clear that the AFL teams were here to stay.

A Born Patriot

It didn't look good for the New England Patriots. It was the 2001 NFL season. The Patriots had lost their starting quarterback to injury. Along came an unimpressive quarterback named Tom Brady.

Who was Tom Brady? At the time, he was a backup quarterback in his second year in the pros waiting patiently for his chance.

Brady had long been waiting for this opportunity. In college at the University of Michigan, he was always battling for the starting quarterback job. He was never sure of his position on the team.

So he took his coach's advice to work on his game. Brady spent his nights staying up late analyzing film. He soon emerged a different player. Brady recognized defenses before the ball was snapped. He became unshakable in the pocket. In the Orange Bowl, he rallied his Wolverines to a 35–34 overtime victory over Alabama.

Still, expectations for Brady in the NFL were low. He wasn't chosen until the sixth round of the NFL Draft. He was the 199th pick overall.

Now, because of an injury to starting quarterback Drew Bledsoe, he was in charge of the offense on an NFL team. But the 0–2 start had put the Patriots into a hole.

Football wasn't the only topic on everyone's mind. On September 11, 2001, terrorists attacked the United States. Football games were postponed. The nation was in mourning. It was an emotional time when football returned the next week.

Many Patriots fans went into the game believing 2001 would be a lost season. The season before, Brady had been a third-stringer. Yet suddenly

TRIPPING TECH

James Madison University quarterback Drew Dudzik bent over center and took the snap. After the first step, he knew he was on his way to a touchdown. It sealed the Dukes' 21–16 victory over Virginia Tech in 2010. "It was like a dream come true when the clock hit zero," said Dukes cornerback Leavander Jones. It was only the second time that a lower division team beat an Associated Press Top 25 team. The first was fifth-ranked Michigan losing to Appalachian State in 2007.

New England Patriots quarterback Tom Brady looks to pass as St. Louis Rams defenders close in during Super Bowl XXXVI.

he could hardly be stopped. New England won 11 of its final 14 games. Then the Patriots won two playoff games to reach the Super Bowl.

It was an amazing run. But it seemed sure to end against the St. Louis Rams in the Super Bowl. The Rams featured one of the greatest offenses the league has ever seen, nicknamed "The Greatest Show on Turf." St. Louis had won the Super Bowl two seasons before. Now the Rams were 14-point favorites to win another one against the Patriots.

Think again. Led by Brady, the Patriots shocked the Rams. The game was tied 17–17 with time expiring in the fourth quarter. Then Patriots kicker Adam Vinatieri made a last-second field goal to secure a 20–17 win.

At 24, Brady became the youngest quarterback in NFL history to win a Super Bowl. When he led the Patriots to two more Super Bowls in the next three years, nobody was calling him an underdog anymore.

Tricks of the Trade

What did the "Statue of Liberty," the "Hook and Ladder," and the "Circus" have in common? The Oklahoma Sooners were about to find out. Those were the names of three trick plays the Boise State University Broncos used to beat the University of Oklahoma in the Fiesta Bowl after the 2006 season.

As part of the high-powered Big 12 Conference, Oklahoma was heavily favored over Boise State. The Sooners were one of college football's top programs. They had won seven national championships and produced 142 All-Americans.

Boise State had dominated the Western Athletic Conference (WAC) for several years. But the WAC was considered a weaker conference than Oklahoma's Big 12.

"We're a group of guys that got overlooked by the Pac-10, Big 12, and Big Ten," said Boise State lineman Jeff Cavender. "We get the cold shoulder. And that's why we play with that chip on our shoulders."

Boise State's Jerard Rabb dives for a touchdown against Oklahoma during the 2007 Fiesta Bowl.

Boise State only wanted some respect from the rest of the football world. They set out to get that respect against Oklahoma.

The Broncos raced to a 14–0 lead. Then they were in trouble. With 18 seconds left in regulation, Boise State trailed 35–28. The Broncos were at midfield facing a fourth-and-18. It was a difficult situation. This was their last chance. They had to move the ball 18 yards or the game would be over.

Quarterback Jared Zabranski saw his backup pretending to juggle. It was the signal for a play called Circus. The hook-and-ladder play tied the game. Now the teams went into overtime.

Once again, the Broncos found themselves in a tough situation. Oklahoma had gone up a touchdown. Boise State would need to score a touchdown and an extra point to stay alive. And to make matters worse, it was fourth and two. Zabranski wasn't happy with his coach. Broncos coach Chris Petersen wanted to run a halfback pass. Zabranski had to serve as a decoy. A player who had not thrown a pass all season, Vinny Perretta, was the man.

It was a perfect pass. Touchdown! The score was 42–41. Still, the Broncos needed the extra point to tie the game and move into a second overtime. Instead they gambled to win.

Enter the Statue of Liberty. The play is a sleight of hand where the quarterback fakes a pass and hands off to a running back. And it worked. Oklahoma was badly fooled. Running back Ian Johnson ran into the end zone for the two-point conversion. Boise State had won, 43–42.

Boise State running back Ian Johnson proposes to his girlfriend after scoring the winning points in the 2007 Fiesta Bowl.

Chapter 3

GREAT INDIVIDUAL UPSETS

An American farm boy against the meanest man in the world. Rulon Gardner vs. Alexander Karelin. Could the American beat the unbeatable Russian at the 2000 Olympic Games in Sydney, Australia?

Karelin was a wrestling giant from Russia. He had never lost in 13 years of international competition. He had three Olympic gold medals and seven world titles. Known for his reverse body lift, he would lift his opponent in the air. Then he would slam him on his head. This earned him a reputation as "the meanest man in the world."

Gardner grew up working on a dairy farm in Wyoming. By fourth grade, he weighed 125 pounds. He was much larger than any of his classmates.

"Fatso," the kids would yell. The teasing and the insults didn't stop.

What did he do? "I used those insults as motivation," Gardner said.

Heavyweight wrestlers Rulon Gardner, *right*, of the United States, and Alexander Karelin of Russia grapple at the 2000 Olympic Games.

He used his size to his advantage. He became a wrestler. He worked hard to increase his strength. He went from an overweight kid to an all-state athlete. When he was 29, he qualified for the 2000 Olympic Games.

In his second bout of the day, he faced the great Karelin. Three years before, Gardner had lost to Karelin by a lopsided 5–0 score in their only meeting. Karelin threw Gardner on his head three times as he slammed him to the ground. Gardner ended up with broken bones in his neck.

So now was the moment for them to meet again. Neither wrestler gained an advantage or scored a point in the first round. In period two, Gardner and Karelin locked together. The wrestlers had to keep their hands clinched. Unexpectedly, Karelin's hands slipped apart. The crowd gasped. Nobody believed what they saw. Gardner received a point. The judges went to the videotape to confirm.

There was a second period for Gardner to finish. Because neither wrestler scored three points, a three-minute overtime was added, too. All Karelin's attempts failed. Gardner held firm.

Wrestler Rulon Gardner celebrates after his shocking gold-medal victory in the 2000 Olympic Games.

Chants of "U-S-A! U-S-A!" filled the arena. As the buzzer sounded signaling Gardner's 1–0 victory, he did a cartwheel in the middle of the mat. The crowd roared. With an American flag over his shoulders, Gardner took a victory lap. One of the greatest upsets in Olympic history was his.

Sarah Hughes of the United States spins her way to a surprising Olympic gold medal at the 2002 Games in Salt Lake City.

Skating Sensation

Michelle Kwan was the favorite going into the figure skating competition at the 2002 Olympic Winter Games in Salt Lake City. The American had won a silver medal four years earlier. And she had claimed all four world championships in women's figure skating from 1996 to 2001. US fans were ready to see the popular skater finally claim Olympic gold.

Expectations weren't as high for fellow American Sarah Hughes. She was a 16-year-old high school student living the dream of her life. She believed she could win an Olympic medal in Salt Lake City. Few believed anyone could overcome Kwan and win the gold, though.

The short program went as planned for Kwan. She ended in first place. Hughes, meanwhile, was disappointed with her fourth place standing. The long program was next. It would determine the medalists.

"There was no pressure on me to win," Hughes said. "I skated for pure enjoyment."

HINGIS HUNG OUT

It was a day Jelena Dokic will always remember. Martina Hingis, too. Dokic whipped Hingis in the first round at Wimbledon in 1999. Why was this so special? Hingis was ranked number one among female tennis players and Dokic was 129th. A Yugoslav-born Australian, Dokic had to win three qualifying matches just to get into the tournament. It was only the third time that the top-seeded woman was eliminated in the first round at Wimbledon. Dokic completed her victory with a 6–2, 6–0 decision in 54 minutes.

And skate she did. The judges and audience loved it. In a lavender dress, Hughes performed two triple-triple jump combinations with perfection. She received a standing ovation that began with her final spin. Hughes jumped from fourth to first. The gold medal was hers. Kwan, one of the most beloved US Olympians of her generation, finished third. She never did win Olympic gold.

Busting Up Iron Mike

Mike Tyson met James "Buster" Douglas for the heavyweight boxing championship of the world in 1990 in Tokyo, Japan.

Tyson was regarded as the best boxer in the world. The heavyweight champion had a 37–0 record with 33 knockouts. Who was Buster Douglas? He was a safe choice for Tyson. The man nicknamed "Iron Mike" figured Douglas would be a quick one-round knockout before moving on to higher profile fighters.

After all, 17 of Tyson's knockouts came in the first round. Tyson had whipped Michael Spinks in 91 seconds and Carl Williams in 93 seconds. He was a menace in the ring, unlike Douglas.

Douglas was an average fighter. He had lost four bouts. In a title fight with Tony Tucker three years earlier, he had fought hard until the tenth round. Then suddenly he seemed to quit. That had happened before in his career. It angered his father, Billy "Dynamite" Douglas. Buster looked up to his father, who was also a fighter. But after the Tucker fight, his father wanted nothing to do with Buster.

PROVING TO BE THE GREATEST

Before he was truly "the greatest"—before he was even Muhammad Ali—he was Cassius Clay, a brash young boxer who liked to tell everyone he was the greatest. Clay had some standing. He had won a gold medal at the 1960 Olympic Games as an amateur. As a pro heavyweight boxer, however, he was still looking for a signature win.

Many believed Clay would finally be humbled in 1964. That year he got a chance to meet Sonny Liston for the world heavyweight title. Liston was a much different fighter than Clay. Nicknamed "The Executioner," he preferred to stand in the ring and slug it out. Clay, meanwhile, was quick on his feet and fast with his fists.

Sportswriters predicted an early knockout by Liston. But in the early rounds, Liston hardly laid a damaging hand on Clay. The underdog flitted in and out of Liston's range. He would pretend to throw a punch. This angered and frustrated the champion. Clay nearly had to quit when a stinging substance got in his eye during the fifth round. But Clay managed to get through the fifth round, and by the end of the sixth the fight was over. The heavyweight ranks had a new champion. The fighter now known as Muhammad Ali was on his way to world fame.

There weren't many chances for the younger Douglas after that. He was having financial problems. He had to borrow money to get gifts the previous Christmas. His mom was sick. His son, Lamar, was ill with leukemia. His family told him to forget boxing and get a job. He was overweight and thinking of quitting boxing.

Then came the call. If Douglas won a fight against Oliver McCall, he would get a title shot with Tyson. Mission accomplished.

Douglas started to train hard for the Tyson fight. This would be his chance to prove himself to his dad. Did Douglas think he was going to beat "the baddest man on the planet?" Everybody expected him to be brutally beaten by Tyson.

The fight was set for February 10, 1990. Just before his trip to Japan, Douglas's mom died. It was a good excuse to quit. But he wouldn't quit. Douglas trained harder than ever.

"I never had a fighter train as hard as Buster did for that one," said Douglas's trainer John Russell.

Yet no one thought he could win. Except those in Douglas's camp. Russell told Douglas he could win if he just got by the first two rounds.

The fight finally arrived. As expected, Tyson came out strong. But Douglas surprisingly survived the first two rounds. He was not afraid of Tyson.

"For once, Tyson wasn't fighting a guy who was afraid of him," said former world champion Evander Holyfield.

In the third round, Douglas peppered Tyson with a left jab. In the fifth, Tyson's left eye began to close. No one in Tyson's corner had remembered to bring ice to slow the swelling. They used a bucket of water.

The champion wasn't finished. In the eighth round, Douglas got careless. A Tyson uppercut sent him crashing to the canvas. At this time, Douglas could have quit. No one would have faulted him. But he wasn't really hurt. He was upset with himself. He listened for the referee's count. When the referee shouted nine, he got up.

Buster Douglas sends Mike Tyson to the canvas in the tenth round of their heavyweight bout in 1990.

"I knew I was winning the fight. When I got hit, it was like, '[dang],'" Douglas said. "But I was fine. When I got up, we looked at each other. The expression on his face told me, 'Oh, no, he got up. I got to keep fighting. The nightmare returns.'"

Two rounds later, Douglas sent Tyson to the canvas. Tyson was helpless; he was in no condition to continue. Douglas had knocked Tyson out at 1:22 of the tenth round. Proudly, Douglas lifted his 11-year-old son Lamar onto his shoulders.

James "Buster" Douglas, not Mike Tyson, was now the center of attention. He was heavyweight champion of the world.

Chapter 4

GREAT BASKETBALL UPSETS

The Cardiac Pack vs. Phi Slamma Jamma. Two college basketball teams with cool nicknames faced each other in the 1983 national championship game.

Led by 7-foot Akeem "The Dream" Olajuwon, it was slam-jam time for the University of Houston Cougars. The Cougars were called Phi Slamma Jamma. Dunking was their game.

The Cardiac Pack was otherwise known as the North Carolina State University Wolfpack. The Wolfpack had lost 10 games during the regular season. They were a middle-of-the-pack Atlantic Coast Conference (ACC) team. They played a number of close games that often weren't decided until the final minute. They had to win the ACC playoffs just to make the National Collegiate Athletic Association (NCAA) Tournament.

Akeem "The Dream" Olajuwon (35) and his Houston Cougars were heavily favored to win the 1983 NCAA title.

That alone was a surprise. In one ACC playoff game, the Wolfpack had to beat Michael Jordan and the University of North Carolina Tar Heels. Then they topped it off by beating Ralph Sampson's University of Virginia team by three points for the league title.

Still, the Wolfpack was an underdog in the NCAA Tournament. With each win in the NCAA Tournament, the Wolfpack became greater underdogs. Yet NC State made it all the way to the final game. The run looked sure to end there, though. The Houston Cougars were one of college basketball's dominant teams. Most favored them to win the national title.

The Wolfpack didn't buy into the hype. And NC State coach Jim Valvano had a plan: Don't allow the Cougars to dunk. The plan seemed to be working. The Wolfpack led the national championship game 33–25 at the half.

Houston wasn't favored for nothing, though. In the second half the Cougars outscored the Wolfpack 17–2 to take the lead. Suddenly, Houston

NO HAWAIIAN VACATION

It happened on the way home from Japan. The nation's top-ranked team made a stopover in Hawaii for a basketball game. It was Christmas 1982. The University of Virginia Cavaliers weren't expecting much of a challenge from little Chaminade University. The Cavs wished they hadn't made the stop. The Silverswords cut up the Cavs, 77–72. Many consider this to be the greatest upset in college basketball history.

Virginia's Ralph Sampson tries unsuccessfully to take the ball from Chaminade's Ernest Pettway in 1982.

NC State players and coach Jim Valvano celebrate the Wolfpack's surprise national championship in 1983.

coach Guy Lewis changed his tactics. He went to a spread offense. That slowed down the game.

Valvano was delighted. He felt he had a good chance to win. And sure enough the Wolfpack caught up. The score was tied 52–52.

NC State called a timeout with 44 seconds to go to set up its final shot. With the clock ticking down under 10 seconds, guard Dereck Whittenburg had the ball. Desperately, he looked around. There was no one to pass to.

With seemingly no other options, Whittenburg put up a shot 35 feet from the basket. It was off the mark—way off. But teammate Lorenzo Charles was standing wide open under the basket.

"I saw Lorenzo get it and dunk it in," Whittenburg said. "And then time ran out. I didn't know what happened. I looked at coach. He looked at me. We didn't know what happened as the buzzer went."

The result lives in history as one of the most famous plays in basketball history. The dunk put NC State up 54–52 and clinched the national title. It was just another nail-biter for the Pack.

"Our kids, they've never quit in a game down the stretch. I knew they wouldn't in the championship," Valvano said.

A Near-Perfect Game

As one of the last teams invited to the 1985 NCAA Tournament, the Villanova University Wildcats had to prove themselves. Their record over a roller coaster season in the Big East Conference was unimpressive. In their last game of the regular season, the Wildcats hardly looked like a playoff team. Big East rival the University of Pittsburgh crushed them.

Fortunately for the Wildcats, the NCAA had expanded the tournament field from 53 to 64 teams. The Wildcats were in. A new window of opportunity presented itself to the Philadelphia school.

However, with strong teams such as North Carolina in their bracket, the Wildcats' chances looked slim. Could they find a way to win? In a shock to many, they did. Villanova won and won and kept winning. Before long the Wildcats found themselves playing the Georgetown University Hoyas in the national championship game.

All eyes were on the Hoyas. They were the national champions the year before. And they had center Patrick Ewing back. The 7-foot superstar was largely considered the best player in the country. His Hoyas were everyone's favorite. They had battled Big East rival St. John's University all season for the number-one ranking. Now they just had to beat Villanova to claim the national title.

A headline in the *Los Angeles Times* summed up the general thought that morning: "It Would Take an N.C. State-Type Miracle to Unseat Hoyas Tonight."

Seemingly everybody doubted that the Wildcats could do it. Everybody, that is, except the Wildcats.

Villanova kept pace with the Hoyas early on. The shot clock was not used in college basketball until the next season. Teams were able to hold the ball as long as they wanted without shooting. It was a tactic known as stalling.

Villanova coach Rollie Massimino's instructed his players to stall. To everyone's amazement, Villanova led Georgetown 29–28 at the half. Their stall-ball offense was working to perfection.

When the Wildcats finally did shoot, most of their shots went in. They made 13 of the 18 they attempted in the first half. The second was even better. The Wildcats only missed one shot in the entire second half on 9-of-10 shooting.

When the buzzer finally sounded, Villanova had held on to win 66–64 in one of the greatest upsets in college basketball history.

"We didn't miss. We couldn't miss," noted Villanova center Ed Pinckney with a smile.

Solid Gold Upset

Rick Barry was basketball's bad boy. To opponents he was either hated, or hated more. To the Golden State Warriors, however, Barry was the golden boy. He led the Warriors into the 1975 National Basketball Association (NBA) playoffs following a 48–34 season.

The Warriors had a problem, though. They lacked inside power. They had a young team with little playoff experience. But they managed to move through the playoffs. Golden State barely survived the Western

Conference finals against the Chicago Bulls. But they did. That set up an NBA Finals series with the Washington Bullets.

In the Eastern Conference, the Bullets had won 60 games. Their power-packed lineup featured All-Stars Elvin Hayes and Wes Unseld. They were among the league's best rebounders. It would give the Bullets an advantage in the inside power game. The Bullets were heavy favorites to win it all.

Barry had other ideas. He was known for having an intense game. Temper tantrums and trash talking were his style. But his star power could not be lessened by his temper. The 6-foot-7 forward was one of the game's great players. He averaged more than 30 points per game and was one of the finest passers of his time.

Few have ever shot free throws better than Barry. He used an unusual underhand shooting technique. But he made an amazing 89 percent of his shots in his 14-year pro career.

"It was a technique I learned from my father," Barry said. "My arms were relaxed at my sides. It gave me an advantage late in the game, when other players were tired and pushed their overhead shots off line."

In the NBA finals, Warriors coach Al Attles called on his reserves to win Game 1, 101–95. Barry sank two free throws in Game 2 to secure a 92–91 win.

The NBA playoffs are a grind. Sixteen of the league's 30 teams qualify. And the seven-game series in each round make upsets very difficult to pull off. Nobody told that to the 2007 Golden State Warriors. They came into the playoffs as the eighth seed in the Western Conference. The top-seeded Dallas Mavericks had their best regular season ever with a 67–15 record. But the Warriors eliminated the Mavericks in six games. Golden State became the first eighth-seeded team to win a seven-game series.

The Warriors were a young team. As their veteran player, Barry had to lead. And his 38 points led to a 109–101 victory in Game 3. Then the Warriors completed the sweep with a 96–95 win in Game 4.

Barry led all scorers in the finals as the Warriors claimed the NBA title. But the sweep had been a total team effort. The dazzling four-game sweep remains one of the greatest surprises in professional sports history.

Three Golden State Warriors defenders surround Washington Bullets center Wes Unseld during the 1975 NBA Finals.

Chapter 5

GREAT BASEBALL UPSETS

In 1969, the United States put a man on the moon. For New York Mets fans, however, the year is best remembered as the year of the "Miracle Mets."

The Mets had been baseball's biggest losers since starting up in 1962. The team's first manager, Casey Stengel, nicknamed them the "Amazin' Mets." For the next seven years, however, the Mets were lovable losers. They finished dead last in the National League (NL) for all but two of those years. Then something magical happened in 1969.

It was a difficult time in the United States. The nation was mourning following the assassinations of politician Robert Kennedy and civil rights leader Martin Luther King Jr. The war in Vietnam was dividing the country. And along came the Mets to create a bright spot.

Ron Swoboda and the New York Mets changed the team's fortunes with a dream season in 1969.

Everybody loves an underdog. Mets manager Gil Hodges—an ex-Marine, an old Brooklyn Dodgers star, and an original Mets player—guided the ultimate underdogs. They shocked the baseball world by winning 100 games. The Mets played that underdog role into the World Series.

New York faced the heavily favored Baltimore Orioles in the Fall Classic. The Orioles had won 109 games. That was more than any team in baseball. Baltimore had the best pitching staff, the best defense, and the best hitting. Sportswriters were calling the Orioles one of the greatest teams in baseball history.

The Orioles were as good as advertised in Game 1. They knocked around Mets ace Tom Seaver. Baltimore won 4–1. It looked like the Mets' "Impossible Dream" season would shortly come to an end.

Not so fast. The Mets responded with a victory in Game 2. Then another in Game 3, highlighted by two amazing catches by outfielder Tommie Agee.

In Game 4, Seaver redeemed himself with a brilliant pitching performance. And once again, the Mets had help from their outfielders. The Mets led 1–0 in the ninth. The Orioles had runners on first and third. Then Brooks Robinson hit a sharp line drive to right-center between Agee and Ron Swoboda.

Swoboda took off with the crack of the bat. "My body was stretched full out," he said.

The ball settled into Swoboda's outstretched glove just inches off the ground. If Swoboda had missed the ball, two runs could have scored. As it was, the Orioles only scored one on Robinson's sacrifice fly. The game went into extra innings tied at 1–1.

The Mets didn't waste any time in the 10th. They quickly scored and won 2–1. They were one game away from the championship. And then it was over. The Mets came back from a 3–0 deficit to win Game 5 by a score of 5–3. They were champions. The Amazin' Mets were now the Miracle Mets.

WALK OFF WINNER

The New York Yankees did everything but beat the Pittsburgh Pirates in the 1960 World Series. They outscored them. They outhit them. They outpitched them. And they still lost. The Pirates won when Bill Mazeroski homered in the bottom of the ninth inning of Game 7.

The New York Mets celebrate at Shea Stadium in New York after beating the Baltimore Orioles in the 1969 World Series.

"They said man would walk on the moon before the New York Mets won the World Series," wrote Jack Lang in the *Long Island Press*. "Man barely beat them."

Miracle Braves

Johnny Evers stepped to the plate for the Boston Braves. It was Game 4 of the 1914 World Series, the Braves against the Philadelphia Athletics. The surprising Braves had won the first three games. The highly favored A's were fighting for their season. One more loss would end it.

It was the best-of-seven series against the A's. The teams were tied at 1–1 in the fifth inning. Evers faced Bob Shawkey. There were two runners on base and two men out.

Crack! Evers swung and connected. The ball sailed into center field for a base hit. In came one run. Then another. The Braves went ahead 3–1. Four innings later, the Braves staked their claim as the World Series champions.

The result shocked the baseball world. Legendary manager Connie Mack's A's featured the famed "$100,000 infield." Their name came from the combined value of their contracts. The A's also had a strong pitching staff. They were considered the best team in baseball. The A's had won four pennants in five seasons.

Leading up to 1914, the Braves had finished last for four of the previous five years. It hadn't looked any better at the start of the 1914 season. By July 4 the Braves were buried in their usual spot in the NL basement. They were a staggering 15 games behind the league-leading New York Giants.

A lot was expected from Bill James, Dick Rudolph, and Lefty Tyler. They were the "Big Three" of the Braves' pitching staff. But all of them struggled through the first half of the season. Then suddenly things turned. The pitchers started to live up to expectations. In a fantastic rush, the Braves climbed steadily to the top of the NL. By the end of the season they had made the biggest comeback in baseball history. They continued to roll into the World Series.

"An aggressive spirit made the Braves a team that didn't know when it was beaten," umpire Billy Evans said.

The Braves made it a four-game sweep. They were in last place on July 4 and World Series champions in October. A ballclub that started the season as a joke had reached the top in a blaze of glory. No one was laughing now.

Beating the Yankees

There was trouble in Miami. It was May 2003. The Florida Marlins had a losing record. Their manager was fired. There were lots of empty seats in the stadium.

The team brought in Jack McKeon as the new manager. It offered a new beginning to the club. What did McKeon tell his players? Play harder. Have fun.

They did, and they soon started winning. By September, the Marlins were in a battle for a wild-card playoff spot. Almost every game was a fight to the end. And with a 91–71 record, Florida indeed claimed that final playoff spot. It was the team's first time in the postseason since winning the 1997 World Series.

The Marlins continued to roll in the postseason. They cruised past the San Francisco Giants three games to one. Then Florida found itself one game away from elimination against the Chicago Cubs. The Marlins survived, and they went on to win the series in seven games. Now they faced the New York Yankees in the World Series.

The Yankees had clinched the American League pennant. That was nothing new. The Yankees had won more championships than any other pro sports team in the United States. The 2003 World Series was their thirty-ninth. Yankee haters had nicknamed the team "The Evil Empire." And the Yankees were at the top of their game in 2003. They had the best record in all of baseball.

The Marlins and Yankees couldn't have been more different. The Marlins were one of baseball's cheapest teams with a payroll of $49 million. The free-spending Yankees spent $153 million. The Yankees were a team of all-stars. Among them were shortstop Derek Jeter, first baseman Jason Giambi, catcher Jorge Posada, and pitchers Roger Clemens, Andy Pettitte, and Mariano Rivera.

The Marlins couldn't compare. Yet they managed to win Game 1 of the Series. The Marlins were giving the Yankees all they could handle. After five games, the Marlins held a 3–2 lead in the Series.

McKeon handed the ball to Josh Beckett for Game 6. The game was at Yankee Stadium, the Bronx Bombers' home turf. Surely, the Yankees would win on their home field.

"You don't want to come in here and watch another team celebrate on your field, that's for sure," Pettitte said.

Fans were nervous. The Yankees hadn't been eliminated on their home field since 1981. But it happened again here. Beckett pitched nine shutout innings. For the second time in just seven years, the Florida Marlins were World Series champions.

Florida Marlins catcher Ivan Rodriguez celebrates with his daughter after beating the New York Yankees in the 2003 World Series.

★ Did you know the term upset was named after a horse? In 1919, a horse named Upset handed Man O' War his only defeat. The term upset became common in sports.

★ The NCAA Tournament expanded to 64 teams in 1985. From then through 2011, a 15th-seeded team had upset a number-two seed only four times. Then, in 2012, it happened twice. It began when Norfolk State beat Missouri 86–84. Then later that day Lehigh beat Duke 75–70.

★ The Oakland Athletics were on the verge of starting a dynasty in the late 1980s. They reached the Fall Classic for the third time in a row in 1990. One year earlier they had swept the crosstown San Francisco Giants in four games. The tables turned in 1990. The Cincinnati Reds stunned Oakland with a four-game sweep of their own. Cincinnati outscored Oakland 22–8.

★ European club soccer is ripe for upsets. That is because many countries have tournaments that include teams from all divisions. The most famous tournament is the Football Association Cup in England. Sometimes powerful Premier League teams have to play against lower-division teams in their small stadiums. And it's not uncommon for the lower-division teams to pull off the upset. One of the most famous upsets was in 2005. Powerhouse Manchester United went on the road to play Exeter City. Exeter was not even within England's top three divisions. Yet the small team held the giants to a 0–0 tie.

GLOSSARY

ACE
The best pitcher on a given baseball team.

AMATEUR
An athlete who is not allowed to earn money through sports.

CONTRACTS
Legal agreements between teams and players that determine the player's salary and commitment to the team.

DRAFT
A system used by professional sports teams to spread incoming talent throughout the league.

HOOK AND LADDER
A football play in which a receiver catches the ball and immediately tosses it to a teammate.

LEUKEMIA
Cancer of the blood cells.

PENNANT
A flag. In baseball it symbolizes that a team won its league championship.

ROOKIE
A player in his first year in a new league.

SACRIFICE FLY
A play in baseball in which a team gives up an out on a fly ball in order to advance a base runner.

SUPREMACY
The top position.

VETERAN
A player who has been playing for a long time.

WILD-CARD
Playoff berths given to the best remaining teams that did not win their respective divisions.

FOR MORE INFORMATION

Selected Bibliography

Gillette, Gary, and Pete Palmer, eds. *The ESPN Baseball Encyclopedia*. 5th ed. New York: Sterling Publishing, 2008.

"Miracle on the Mat." *CNN Sports Illustrated*. CNN/Sports Illustrated. 14 Nov. 2000. Web. 15 March 2013.

Wright, Frank L. *The Ultimate Basketball Book*. Crystal Bay, NV: Sierra Vista Publications, 2007.

Further Readings

Berman, Len. *The Greatest Moments in Sports: Upsets and Underdogs*. Naperville, IL: Sourcebooks Jabberwocky, 2012.

Krantz, Les. *Dark Horses & Underdogs: The Greatest Sports Upsets of All Time*. New York: Warner Books, 2005.

McCarthy, John. *Starry Knights: The 1963 College All-Stars and the Forgotten Story of Football's Greatest Upset*. San Diego, CA: Aventine Press, 2009.

Wilner, Barry, and Ken Rappoport. *Miracles, Shockers, and Long Shots: The Greatest Sports Upsets of All Time*. Lanham, MD: Taylor Trade, 2006.

Web Links

To learn more about the biggest upsets in sports, visit ABDO Publishing Company online at **www.abdopublishing.com**. Web sites about the biggest upsets in sports are featured on our Book Links page. These links are routinely monitored and updated to provide the most current information available.

Places to Visit

Naismith Memorial Basketball Hall of Fame
1000 Hall Fame Ave
Springfield, MA 01105
(413) 781-6500
www.hoophall.com
The Naismith Memorial Basketball Hall of Fame honors basketball's greatest players and moments.

National Baseball Hall of Fame and Museum
25 Main Street
Cooperstown, NY 13326
(888) 425-5633
www.baseballhall.org
This hall of fame and museum highlights the greatest players and moments in the history of baseball.

Pro Football Hall of Fame
2121 George Halas Drive NW
Canton, OH 44708
(330) 456-8207
www.profootballhof.com
This hall of fame and museum highlights the greatest players and moments in the history of the NFL.

INDEX

Ali, Muhammad, 35
Appalachian State, 18, 22

Baltimore Colts, 19–21
Baltimore Orioles, 52–53
Barry, Rick, 46–48
Boise State University, 24–26
Borghi, Frank, 12
Boston Braves, 55–57
Brady, Tom, 21–24

Canada, 15
Chaminade University, 40
Charles, Lorenzo, 43
Colombia, 10
Craig, Jim 8

Dallas Mavericks, 48
Dokic, Jelena, 33
Dominican Republic, 52
Douglas, James "Buster," 34–37
Edmonton Oilers, 13–15
England, 8–13
Eruzione, Mike, 7–8
Evers, Johnny, 55

Florida Marlins, 57–58

Gaetjens, Joe, 11
Gardner, Rulon, 28–31
George Mason University, 46

Georgetown University, 44–46
Golden State Warriors, 46–48
Granato, Cammi, 15
Gretzky, Wayne, 13

Hingis, Martina, 33
Hughes, Sarah, 33–34

James Madison University, 22
Johnson, Ian, 26

Kansas City Chiefs, 21
Karelin, Alexander, 28–30
Kwan, Michelle, 33–34

Lacoste, Catherine, 30
Liston, Sonny, 35
Los Angeles Kings, 13–15

Mazeroski, Bill, 53
"Miracle on Ice," 4–8
"Miracle on Grass," 8–13
"Miracle on Manchester," 13–15

Namath, Joe, 16–21
Netherlands, 52
New England Patriots, 21–24
New York Jets, 16–21
New York Mets, 50–54
New York Yankees, 53, 57–58
North Carolina State, 38–43, 44

Olympic Games, 4–8, 15, 28–34
Ortiz, David, 52

Philadelphia Athletics, 55
Pittsburgh Pirates, 53

Soviet Union, 4–8
St. Louis Rams, 23–24
Stewart, Earnie, 10

Team USA, 4–13, 15
Tyson, Mike, 34–37

University of Alabama, 16, 22
University of Connecticut, 46
University of Houston, 38–43
University of Michigan, 18, 21, 22
University of Oklahoma, 24–26
University of Virginia, 40

Valvano, Jim, 40, 43
Villanova University, 43–46
Virginia Tech, 22

Washington Bullets, 47–48
World Baseball Classic, 52
World Cup, 8–13

About the Author

Ken Rappoport is a professional sportswriter with more than 60 books to his credit in both the adult and young readers fields. Working for the Associated Press in New York for 30 years, he wrote about every major sport and was AP's national hockey writer for 14 seasons. Rappoport has been cited for his work in the young adult field and has written extensively for magazines.